AUDREY

THE AMAZING INVENTOR

D1349659

RV – To Ma and Pa, with love and many thanks.
KW – For Rob, Sophie, David and Mike. With love.

Quarto is the authority on a wide range of topics.
Quarto educates, entertains and enriches the lives of
our readers—enthusiasts and lovers of hands-on living.
www.quartoknows.com

© 2018 Quarto Publishing plc

Text © Rachel Valentine

Illustrations © Katie Weymouth

Rachel Valentine has asserted her right to be identified as the author of this work.

Katie Weymouth has asserted her right to be identified as the illustrator of this work.

First Published in 2018 by words & pictures,

an imprint of The Quarto Group.

The Old Brewery, 6 Blundell Street,

London N7 9BH, United Kingdom.

T (0)20 7700 6700 F (0)20 7700 8066

www.quartoknows.com

No part of this publication may be reproduced, stored in a retrieval system, or transmitted in any form,

or by any means, electrical, mechanical, photocopying, recording or otherwise, without the prior written

permission of the publisher or a licence permitting restricted copying. In the United Kingdom such licences

are issued by the Copyright Licensing Agency, Barnards Inn, 86 Fetter Lane, London EC4A 1EN.

All rights reserved.

A catalogue record for this book is available from the British Library.

ISBN: 978-1-91027-758-4

9 8 7 6 5 4 3 2 1

Manufactured in Shenzhen, China

South Lanarkshire Library Service	
BL	
C70261372/	
Askews & Holts	
JN	£11.99
5913104	

MIX
Paper from
responsible sources
FSC® C101537
FSC
www.fsc.org

words & pictures

AUDREY
THE AMAZING INVENTOR

written by **Rachel Valentine**
illustrated by **Katie Weymouth**

Audrey was the most inquisitive
girl you could hope to meet.

She never stopped asking questions and searching for answers.

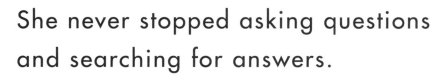

And she loved to fiddle and find out how everything worked.

So the day Audrey's teacher asked
the class, "What do you want to
be when you grow up?"
Audrey beamed...

She would invent AMAZING things.
But where to begin?

Amazing fun things to cheer up Happy Cat?
Amazing useful things for Daddy?

Audrey began to invent at a rapid rate.

The egg collector made Daddy's
mornings much easier...

...until it didn't!

The cat-a-pult was very impressive...

...although it wasn't Happy Cat's favourite idea!

In fact, neither Happy Cat nor Daddy seemed
very keen on Audrey's inventions.
Which were...

...amazingly scary!

...amazingly messy!

...and sometimes
just amazingly wrong!

As for the strawberry
jam dispenser...

"Oh, Happy Cat," sighed Audrey.
"Being an inventor isn't easy."
But, as Audrey stroked his sticky fur,
she had another spark of an idea.
Maybe this one would work?

She ran to the shed and banged,
clattered and battered.

 Then she laid out a trail of fishy treats, which Happy Cat followed straight into...

...the cat wash.

It bubbled...

and bubbled...

and
bubbled...

"No!" cried Audrey. "Stop bubbling!"

But the bubbles went everywhere.
Happy Cat wasn't happy.
Daddy wasn't happy.

And Audrey was utterly miserable.

"I'm the world's worst inventor!" she wailed.

Later, when Daddy came to kiss her goodnight, he said, "I don't expect inventors ever get it right the first time." "But ALL my inventions are disasters," Audrey replied. "They're not disasters, so long as you learn from them," smiled Daddy. "You just need to keep trying!"

That made Audrey feel much better. And, before long,
a glimmer of a thought began to grow in her mind.
The thought grew and grew, until it exploded into
an idea. The most amazing idea ever!

But this time Audrey was going to plan – really plan. For days she thought, sketched, measured and wrote lists.

She gathered exactly the right materials.

And carefully, ever so carefully, she began to saw, hammer, glue and tape.

She tested her invention again and again. And at long last it was ready!

Daddy couldn't wait to see it, but Audrey grinned, "Not until morning!"

As the sun rose, Audrey yawned, stretched and rolled over in bed. Then she dropped a marble,

which knocked
a domino,
which fell on
a spring,

which sprang down the
stairs and hit two balls.
One woke Daddy – POP!
One hit a lever – PING!
It started a train,

which tooted and rumbled,
and whirred a wheel,
which cranked
up a chain...

...and breakfast was served!

"Wow! How utterly amazing!" Daddy gasped.

"And now for the best bit..." said Audrey.

But...
CLUNK!
The fishy treat chute bulged and shook.
"Oh no!" groaned Audrey,
"Another disaster!"

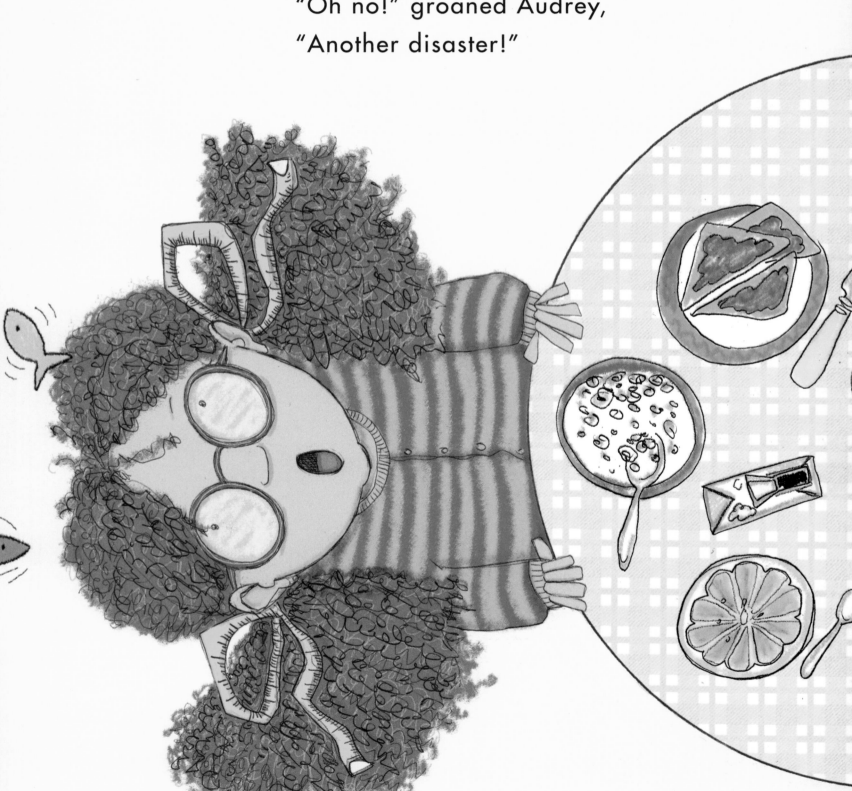

But this time, Happy Cat didn't mind one bit!